STEP FORWARD WITH
INTEGRITY

SHANNON WELBOURN

Crabtree Publishing Company

www.crabtreebooks.com

STEP FORWARD!

Author
Shannon Welbourn

Series research and development
Reagan Miller

Editorial director
Kathy Middleton

Editors
Reagan Miller, Janine Deschenes

Series Consultant
Larry Miller: BA (Sociology), BPE, MSc.Ed
Retired teacher, guidance counselor, and certified coach

Print and production coordinator
Katherine Berti

Design and photo research
Katherine Berti

Photographs
Wikimedia: p 8 (inset)
The Be ONE Project: Matthew Kaplan: p 17
Other images by Shutterstock

Library and Archives Canada Cataloguing in Publication

Welbourn, Shannon, author
    Step forward with integrity / Shannon Welbourn.

(Step forward!)
Includes index.
Issued in print and electronic formats.
ISBN 978-0-7787-2788-0 (hardback).--ISBN 978-0-7787-2828-3 (paperback).--
ISBN 978-1-4271-1832-5 (html)

    1. Integrity--Juvenile literature. I. Title.

BJ1533.I58W45 2016   j179'.9   C2016-903361-9
                                              C2016-903362-7

Library of Congress Cataloging-in-Publication Data

Names: Welbourn, Shannon, author.
Title: Step forward with integrity / Shannon Welbourn.
Description: New York : Crabtree Publishing Company, [2017] |
  Series: Step forward! | Includes index.
Identifiers: LCCN 2016034719 (print) | LCCN 2016043369 (ebook) |
  ISBN 9780778727880 (reinforced library binding : alk. paper) |
  ISBN 9780778728283 (pbk. : alk. paper) |
  ISBN 9781427118325 (Electronic HTML)
Subjects: LCSH: Integrity--Juvenile literature.
Classification: LCC BJ1533.I58 W45 2017 (print) | LCC BJ1533.I58 (ebook) |
  DDC 179/.9--dc23
LC record available at https://lccn.loc.gov/2016034719

Crabtree Publishing Company

www.crabtreebooks.com   1-800-387-7650

Printed in Canada/102016/IH20160811

Published in Canada
Crabtree Publishing
616 Welland Ave.
St. Catharines, Ontario
L2M 5V6

Published in the United States
Crabtree Publishing
PMB 59051
350 Fifth Avenue, 59th Floor
New York, New York 10118

Published in the United Kingdom
Crabtree Publishing
Maritime House
Basin Road North, Hove
BN41 1WR

Published in Australia
Crabtree Publishing
3 Charles Street
Coburg North
VIC 3058

CONTENTS

WHAT IS INTEGRITY?

"He is a person of integrity." When you hear a person described this way, do you know what it means?

Integrity is doing the right thing even when no one is watching. It means doing what you say you are going to do. It also means staying true to your beliefs. Everyone can develop integrity. To do so, you must first understand your beliefs of right and wrong. Your **morals** and **values** have an effect on your integrity. A value is something a person strongly believes. For example, being honest is a value. A moral is a principle, or rule, that someone follows in their life. Your morals help you determine what you think is right and wrong. Integrity means you do what you know is right, even if things are difficult.

When you live your life with integrity, you are staying true to your morals and values. You keep your word and do what is right.

WHY IS INTEGRITY IMPORTANT?

Understanding your own beliefs is important. When you understand your morals and values, you can build integrity.

Integrity develops from making good choices. You use your personal values to make choices. Consider your values and how they affect the choices you make. Personal values shape your behavior. They often form from your family's beliefs and values. They can also form from what your peers believe. Your values become **standards**. For example, if cooperation is one of your values, you will strive to work well with others. When people use integrity to act and make decisions based on their beliefs, they are less likely to regret their choices.

These children are working together to help fix their friend's bike. This shows the value of helping others.

JOEY PRUSAK

One way to show integrity is to help others by standing up for what is right. That's what teenager Joey Prusak did at the local Dairy Queen where he worked.

Name: Joey Prusak

From: Minneapolis, Minnesota

Accomplishment: Showed integrity by staying true to his beliefs and standing up for what is right

One day, one of his regular customers came in for ice cream. This customer had a **visual impairment** and did not notice he dropped a $20 bill while leaving the store. Joey saw this happen but before he could call out to the man, a woman picked up the money. Joey thought the woman was going to do the right thing and return it to the man. But instead she took the money and came to the front counter to order ice cream.

Joey told the woman that he saw her take the money. He told her to return the money to the man or he would not serve her. She refused, and Joey asked her to leave the store. Joey then gave the man $20 of his own money to replace the money the woman took. Joey made a choice that shows he stayed true to his values. His story quickly spread online and serves as a good example of integrity.

STEP FURTHER

What other choices could Joey have made in this situation?

INTEGRITY AT HOME

Community

School

Home

How you behave at home is important to your family. Showing integrity means that you respect **your family members.**

Your family members need to know they can trust you. You need to be **reliable**. People with integrity follow through on what is asked of them, even when no one is watching. Your parents give you the responsibility of feeding the family dog. You are about to leave for your baseball game when you notice his water dish is empty. You take the time to fill the dish before leaving. This shows integrity because you followed through on your **commitment** to feed your dog, even when you were on your way out the door and no one was around. And your dog will be thankful too!

One way to show your integrity is following through on what you say you're going to do. Finishing your chores before playing outside shows integrity.

INTEGRITY AT SCHOOL

Community

School

Home

Acting with integrity involves doing the right thing and being responsible **for your actions.**

Being a dependable student means that you do the things that are expected of you. Coming to school prepared and ready to learn, and trying your best in class, shows your integrity.

*Taking **responsibility** for your actions is a way that you can show integrity. When you don't finish homework, you may have to stay in at recess.*

Having integrity means you should act or behave in a certain way. Your classmates and teacher need to know you will follow classroom rules, such as raising your hand to speak or treating peers with respect. Working in a group with other people means each of you agrees to do one part of a project. Each person needs to be responsible. Acting with integrity means that you follow your word and complete your part.

STEP FURTHER

What would you do if a friend asks to copy your answers on a test?

If you do not do your part in a group project, it will hurt others.

MATTHEW KAPLAN

Name: Matthew Kaplan

From: Phoenix, Arizona

Accomplishment: Founded the Be O.N.E. Project to encourage integrity in students and stop bullying

When Matthew Kaplan discovered that his younger brother, Josh, was being bullied, he decided to stand up for his values and make a difference.

Matthew founded the Be O.N.E. Project, which stands for Be Open to New Experiences. His project encourages kids to act with integrity. Matthew felt that many kids who were bullying others did not realize how their actions were hurting these people. He believes that if all kids develop their morals and values and stay true to them, school communities can become more **inclusive** and positive for everyone. The Be O.N.E. Project encourages kids to **reflect** on how their actions affect others. Kids also reflect on whether their actions follow their values, and take responsibility if they were involved in bullying.

> "The solution lies in teaching students that we have the power to shape the culture in our schools."
>
> —Matthew Kaplan

Matthew visits schools and encourages kids to be role models for one another by being kind and accepting to everyone, even when no one is watching. He also encourages kids to hold each other **accountable** for their actions. This means that kids in a school community hold each other responsible for acting with integrity. Matthew hopes that with a little integrity, students can work together to make their school communities safe, accepting, and positive places for everyone.

In 2014, Matthew won the Disney "Hero for Change" award for his anti-bullying work. He values being accepting to everyone, and stands up for that value every day. That's integrity in action!

OVERCOMING CHALLENGES

Acting with integrity is not always easy. It can be difficult. You can work on building integrity throughout your life.

Sometimes we know what the right thing to do is, but we find it hard to do. It can be challenging to build integrity when we are tempted to play video games instead of following through on our commitment to finish our chores. Showing integrity can also be difficult when it seems easier to tell a lie than to be honest, such as telling your teacher that a dog ate your homework instead of telling the truth that you did not complete it. Even though it's not always easy, it's important to stay true to our values and practice integrity!

Remember the tips below to help keep your integrity in check.

Be honest, trustworthy, and reliable.

Keep your values in mind.

Always take responsibility for your actions.

Always do what you believe is right.

Think about how your actions will affect others.

Follow your word. If you said you would do something, do it.

ENCOURAGING INTEGRITY IN OTHERS

Promote integrity in your daily life by helping others stay true to their values, too.

Be a good example to your friends and others around you. Living your life with integrity shows others the type of person you are. People learn they can trust you. They know that you are reliable. Encourage others to act with honestly and fairness. Help them to understand how their decisions and actions build their character. Encourage others to act with integrity. Help them think about their morals and values and be true to their beliefs, no matter what.

When you treat others with kindness, honesty, and integrity, you receive much of the same in return.

STEP
FURTHER

Write a list of your values. How can you show others your integrity by upholding what you believe?

INTEGRITY IN ACTION

In this book, you have learned why integrity is important and some of the ways people show it in their daily lives.

Read each of the examples and decide if the person's actions show integrity.

If you answer yes, explain your thinking.

If you answer no, describe how the person could change their actions to show integrity.

Sonya breaks her friend's toy by mistake. Her friend doesn't see her break it, so Sonya puts the toy back without telling her.

Dominic notices the new girl in his class has no one to play with during recess. He thinks about asking her to play tag with him and his friends. He decides to wait for someone else to play with her instead.

Malik has been on time for every swimming practice this summer. Today he lost track of time and arrived ten minutes late. He tells his coach he is sorry and will work hard to try to be on time next week.

LEARNING MORE

BOOKS

Graves, Sue. *I Didn't Do It!: A book about telling the truth.* Free Spirit Publishing, 2013

Guillain, Charlotte. *The Empty Pot: A Chinese Folk Tale.* Raintree, 2014.

Meiners, Cheri J. & Allen, Elizabeth. *Stand Tall!: A book about integrity.* Free Spirit Publishing, 2015

WEBSITES

www.goodcharacter.com
Character education for teachers and their students.

www.inspiremykids.com
A place for kids to find age-appropriate, real-life stories and inspiration toward positive action.

www.kidsnowcanada.org
A program that helps students learn positive choices and develop life skills needed for success.

WORDS TO KNOW

accountable [*uh*-KOUN-t*uh*-b*uh* l] adjective To take responsibility for actions

commitment [k*uh*-MIT-m*uh* nt] noun A promise to do something

inclusive [in-KLOO-siv] adjective Describing a group or space that is accepting or welcoming to all

morals [MAWR-*uh* ls] noun Practices or beliefs held by a person, based on what is believed to be right and wrong

reflect [ri-FLEKT] verb To think back on something

reliable [ri-lahy-*uh*-b*uh* l] noun The ability to be depended on for honesty

respect [ri-SPEKT] verb The act of giving something or someone the attention it deserves

responsibility [ri-spon-s*uh*-BIL-t-tee] noun Being accountable, or taking blame, for a commitment made

responsible [ri-SPON-suh-buhl] adjective Reliable or dependable

standards [STAN-derds] noun Morals, ethics, and values that determine thoughts and behaviors

values [VAL-yoo] noun Things or qualities held to high esteem, or having importance to a person

visual impairment [VIZH-oo-*uh*l im-PAIR-m*uh* nt] noun Having difficulty seeing

INDEX

ABOUT THE AUTHOR

Shannon Welbourn is a freelance author of educational K-12 books. She holds an honors BA in Child & Youth Studies, and is a certified teacher. Shannon works full-time as a Library and Media Specialist. In this position, she works closely with teachers and teacher candidates, helping to inspire and develop a passion for learning. Shannon lives close to Niagara Falls and enjoys vacationing in the Muskokas with her family.